The Hands-On Workbook for ADHD Children

100 Empowering Activities to Build Successful Skills

Richard Bass

2 FREE Bonuses!

Receive a FREE Planner for Kids and a copy of the Positive Discipline Playbook by scanning below!

Table of Contents

Introduction

"Picture a room with 1,000 TV's with each TV showing something different. Now try and concentrate on just one TV without getting distracted."

–Damian DaViking Aird

What screams, "I have a child with ADHD?" without actually saying it?

How about sending your child upstairs to bring down laundry, and 15 minutes later, find them sitting on the floor, carefully examining their socks?

Or sitting down with your child to do homework—except you are the only person sitting down (waiting for them to complete their 10th jumping jack before going back to practicing spelling)?

Or how about constantly having to hear, "I'm bored," despite all of the suggestions you have given your child on how to spend their time?

People often say you have your hands full when commenting on your child's hyperactivity. But the truth of the matter is they have no idea just how much physical and mental stimulation your child needs!

You can have a fun activity planned out for the weekend, but woe to you if you have only organized one, or don't have a plan B in case your idea of "fun" isn't necessarily fun for your kid.

Parenting a child with attention-deficit/hyperactivity disorder (ADHD) can sometimes feel exhausting because they constantly need something to do. And when they aren't actively working on something, they can get irritable, restless, and find unproductive ways to keep busy.

As a parent, you won't always know how to satiate your child's need for action. Between work, parenting other kids, and running the household, there will be times when you go blank and can't think of an effective plan on how to keep your child engaged. Fortunately, this workbook has done most of the legwork for you, presenting 100 different ways to help your child burn off extra energy and learn useful skills along the way.

These activities are suitable for children between 3-10 years old, and they cover a range of skills, such as movement, problem-solving, concentration, organization, self-soothing, self-awareness, and much more! Some activities require your hands-on assistance, while others can be done independently. After going through this workbook with your child, you will feel more prepared to respond to their constant need for stimulation.

Chapter 1:

Move Your Body

"It is difficult to instruct children because of their natural inattention; the true mode, of course, is to first make our modes interesting to them."

–John Locke

Why ADHD Kids Need to Stay Active

Physical activity is one of the best ways to burn some of your child's energy in a productive way. Research has shown that children with ADHD need to move to assist them in learning (MacDonald, 2015). Repetitive movements like fidgeting, swinging legs, tapping feet, or rocking can be instrumental in problem-solving and memorizing information. This doesn't mean that you should let your child run wild around the house, but you do need to help them focus their energy on rewarding physical activities. The following section includes fun and rewarding exercises to get your child moving.

Physical Activities to Keep Your Kid Moving

The best kinds of physical activity for your child are those that increase their heart rate. Even though your child gets plenty of opportunities to increase their heart rate away from home, whether it be running on the playground during recess, taking a swimming class, or riding their bike outside, they are often still buzzing when they get home.

Depending on your child's age, the type of activities they can perform will differ. For example, active unstructured playing or adult-facilitated play for three hours a day is sufficient for a preschooler. Older kids, ranging between 6-10 years old will benefit from 60 minutes of moderate to intense physical activity three times per week. Here are 10 fun physical activities to keep your child moving:

1. **Dancing**

Create a playlist of up-tempo songs and encourage your child to dance along with you. If you have an older child, you can watch a dance tutorial online and follow along. Tailor the genre of music to suit your child's music tastes, so they can enjoy the experience.

2. **Hot Lava Floor**

Imagine that the playroom floor has suddenly turned into hot smoldering lava. Your challenge is to get from one safe patch of "land" to the next without sinking into the lava. Before the game starts, grab a few pieces of clothing that represent safe patches of land and lay them across the floor. Cross the room first and encourage your child to follow after you.

3. **Hopscotch**

Find a hard surface in your front or backyard that you can turn into your hopscotch court. Using paint or chalk, create the traditional hopscotch diagram (if you are playing inside, you can use masking tape).

Add numbers to your diagram, numbering the blocks from one to 10. Challenge your child to count the blocks while hopping across the course, alternating between using one and both legs.

4. **Martial Arts**

Martial arts is a fun physical activity that teaches your child different moves and keeps them active. Other skills that can be learned through martial arts are self-control, balance, timing, concentration, and fine motor skills.

There are different types of martial arts classes that you can enroll your child in, including karate, taekwon-do, judo, or jiu jitsu. Each type focuses on a specific skill. For example, karate teaches focus and self-defense, while taekwon-do teaches self-discipline and self-control. Do your research and find one that offers your kid the most value!

5. **Strength Training**

For older kids who need more of a physical challenge, strength training can be a fun way to keep them engaged. The definition of strength training is any physical activity that uses body weight to strengthen muscles. Below is a list of strength training exercises you can incorporate into your child's at-home workout:

- Push-ups

- Squats

- Squat jumps

- Lunges

- Planks

- Burpees

- Sit-ups

- Jumping jacks

- Cartwheels

- Handstand against a wall

While this form of exercise is safe, it is not suitable for all children. According to the American Academy of Pediatrics, children with health conditions like high blood pressure, heart disease, history of cancer, or seizure disorders should consult a doctor before performing strength training exercises (Dreisbach, 2022).

6. Basic Yoga

Yoga is a relaxing physical activity that helps children slow their breathing, improve balance, and increase mental clarity. Studies have shown that when practiced regularly (about twice per week), yoga can reduce the severity of ADHD symptoms, as well as improve a child's ability to pay attention in the classroom (Cohen et al., 2018).

To get started with yoga, both you and your child will need loose-fitting comfortable clothes and enough floor space to move without any obstructions (having yoga mats is a bonus). There are many free yoga instructional videos online, like the YouTube channel Cosmic Kids, geared toward smaller children, with easy-to-follow instructions.

7. Balance Beam

This fun physical activity can be played indoors or out. All you will need is masking tape or chalk, depending on your flooring. Make a straight line on the ground and challenge your child to walk on it until they reach the end. The goal is to keep their feet on the line and avoid stumbling over it.

For older children, you can increase the stakes by making several lines at different angles, drawing spirals rather than straight lines, or setting a timer to see how fast they can complete the course.

8. Up in the Air

If your kid can't play outside, you can bring the adventure indoors by playing this fun game. Blow up a balloon and challenge your child to keep tapping it in the air, so that it doesn't fall to the ground. Even though this game can be played alone, it is double the fun when played by a group of children. Just a heads up—you may want to remove obstructions laying on the floor and any fragile objects!

9. Hot Potato

Another exciting game for a group of children is hot potato! Create a soft ball out of a few pairs of socks. Tell your children to pretend the ball is a hot potato. Position the kids in a circle and tell them to throw the hot potato to each other, moving as quickly as possible.

Older kids may want more of a challenge. Incorporate an element of musical chairs by playing music and stopping the song randomly. Whoever is holding the hot potato when the song stops is out!

10. Follow the Leader

Do you have a small child who cannot sit still? Why not play follow the leader? Pretend that you are a military general and your child is a soldier. They are instructed to go wherever the general goes, and do whatever the general does—no questions asked! If you are sweeping the kitchen, hand them a second broom and sweep together. When it is time to fold the laundry, the soldier folds with you. Add a few surprise tasks to keep the soldier engaged, like doing jumping jacks or dipping into the kiddie pool.

Coloring Break

Chapter 2:

Let's Get Organized

"In the ADHD home, ease of stowage takes precedence over ease of retrieval. Give everything a 'home.'"

–Susan C. Pinsky

Making Organization Fun!

While ADHD medication can improve your child's ability to stay organized, they still need that extra push from you and their teachers to turn organizational skills into habits. The key to teaching your child how to stay organized is to incorporate basic planning, cleaning, and organizational skills into their play. This will ensure that they get regular practice and find it easy-peasy to follow the systems you create together! Below are clever and fun activities that teach organizational skills.

Activities to Improve Organizational Skills

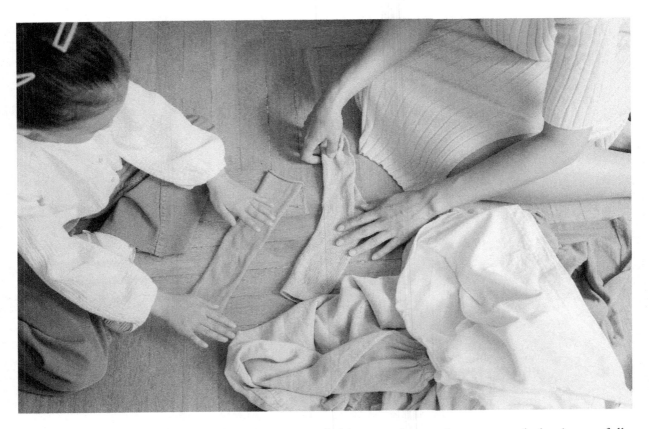

If you are parenting a child with ADHD, you probably get exhausted at constantly having to follow behind your child and keep your home organized. Fortunately for you, there are interactive ways of teaching your child how to follow systems and complete small household tasks. Here are 10 great ways to help your child improve their organization skills:

1. **Attack the Clutter**

When your child has a short attention span, time-based games can be a lot of fun! Choose an area, room, or drawer in the house that needs to be cleaned out. Set the timer for a certain number of minutes and challenge your kid to throw out as many items as possible. Have a large empty container on hand to collect items that are being thrown away.

2. Laundry Race

If you have an older child, create a laundry folding competition and race to see who can fold the most clothes—as neatly as possible—within a limited amount of time. When the timer goes off, count how many items each of you were able to fold. Have an awesome prize waiting for the winner.

3. Fill a Basket With Toys

Spend an afternoon cleaning up the playroom by playing a game of who can fill their basket with the most toys. You can use two empty laundry baskets or storage containers—one for you and one for your child. Once again, set a timer, or better yet, play some up-tempo background music to liven the mood!

4. Scavenger Hunt

Imagine that you and your child are detectives looking for specific dirty clothes, unused objects, or trash around the house. You can choose whether to clean up existing clutter or purposely place items around the house. Provide simple clues, riddles, or pictures (or a combination of all three) to help them find the items. Once the items are found, ask your child to put them back in their normal spot (e.g., a ball found in the bathroom needs to be returned to the garden).

5. Pantry Takeover

Move the action to the kitchen and ask your child to help you organize the pantry. There are a variety of ways you can neatly pack food items. For example, you can sort items by shape, color, groups of food, or matching containers. Choose an option that will be the easiest for your child to work with.

6. Mannequin Challenge

Whenever you are sorting through your child's closet, find a way to involve them by playing the mannequin challenge. Have your child pose like a mannequin while you have them try on clothes to see what they have outgrown the items. Make it fun by playing music in the background, taking photos of them, or asking them to wear various accessories.

7. Donation Drive

Take two big cardboard boxes and place them in your child's room. Ask them to take all of their clothes and throw them on the floor. Help them sort through their clothes and place them inside the "Keep" or "Donate" box. Schedule a visit to your local shelter and drop the clothes off with your child.

8. Create Colorful Storage Bins

One of the ways to teach your child the importance of putting things away is to designate specific containers for their toys and crafts. Containers can come in all types of shapes and sizes, ranging from plastic shoe boxes to large bins. Find containers suitable for your child's possessions and have fun decorating them together. Afterward, have them choose where to place the container and the items that go inside.

9. Create a Shopping List

Before going out to run errands, sit down with your child and create a shopping list. If you are running to the grocery store, for example, ask them to help you brainstorm food items to buy. Have them walk into the pantry and open the refrigerator to see what foods are missing or nearly depleted. If they are old enough, supervise them while they create the list on their own.

10. Spot the Difference

A fun way to help an older child learn how to keep their room tidy is to play a game of spot the difference. Walk them through a neat bedroom and point out a maximum of five things that make the room tidy. For example, you might mention the made bed, clean floors, and drawn-back curtains. Then, ask them to go inside their room and spot the differences. For everything they tidy up, give them a reward!

Coloring Break

Chapter 3:

Explore the Garden

"Their minds were not built to sit and be taught. They were built to explore, play, and learn."

–Layla Gordon Lu

Go Outside!

Did you know that outdoor play can reduce the symptoms of ADHD in children? Studies have shown that children with ADHD who play outside often are happier, smarter, and less stressed. Moreover, since outdoor activities incorporate an element of physical exercise, higher amounts of dopamine are produced in the brain, which contributes to better moods and sharper cognitive functioning. Below are 10 outdoor activities that you can enjoy with your child.

Interactive Outdoor Activities for Kids

Like any parent, you probably have a few choice words to say about the takeover of technology in your home. Ideally, you would like your kid to spend more time exploring the great outdoors rather than spending hours staring at a smartphone, computer or TV screen. With some encouragement and fun playtime suggestions, you can inspire your kid to enjoy outdoor activities! Here are 10 adventurous activities to enjoy outdoors:

1. Do Some Garden Clean Up

Gardening offers your child an opportunity to get in touch with nature and learn how to take responsibility for something. Find small garden jobs that you can do with your child, such as picking up twigs, watering plants, or planting new seeds.

2. Decorate Stones

Do you have small- to medium-sized stones in your garden? Ask your child to collect a few stones that are different shapes and sizes. Set the stones on a disposable sheet of large paper and bring out your assortment of paints. Create a few examples of decorative stones that your child can use as inspiration. Then, sit back and watch their imaginations go wild!

3. Create a Leaf Collage

Hand your child an empty bag and ask them to collect a bunch of fallen leaves. Empty the bag on a flat surface and sort them into groups of different colors or shades. Next, you will need a medium-sized piece of paper and craft glue. Show your child how to glue and press the different leaves on the paper, closing as many white gaps as possible. Allow the glue to set for about an hour before picking up the piece of paper.

4. Have a Picnic

When the weather is sunny, enjoy your lunch outside. You can make your picnic as simple or as fancy as you want—just be sure to include plenty of good food and a few short stories to read to your child.

5. Play "I Spy"

Although the game is simple, I Spy tests your child's descriptive and cognitive skills. You and your child can take turns identifying interesting objects in the garden. The first player starts off by giving a clue, "I spy with my little eye something …," which could be the color or shape of the object or the first letter of the word. Add a physical element to the activity by running to fetch the object and bringing it back to the base.

6. Create a Garden Kitchen

This activity requires a little bit of do-it-yourself (DIY) skill before the actual fun begins. You can create a garden kitchen using recycled pieces of wood (to build furniture pieces) and other safe garden tools you don't use anymore. Ask your child to imagine they are preparing a meal for you in their garden kitchen. Encourage them to explore the garden to find interesting ingredients for the dish, like dirt, spoiled flowers, and water from the tap. Not only will this activity keep them focused and thoroughly entertained, it will also engage their senses and make them feel calm.

7. Make a Campfire

If you have older children, a great way to get them outside is to ask them to help you make a campfire. For safety reasons, they should do more assisting than taking the lead for this activity. You can turn this activity into an educational opportunity to teach them about the science of making fire (i.e., the elements of the fire triangle) or create a warm and cozy atmosphere for the family to bond. Keep your child entertained by reading a book or making delicious s'mores!

8. Bubble-Blowing Competition

Warning: This activity will cause a lot of giggling! Blowing bubbles is a stress-relieving, fun activity that can be enjoyed indoors and out. You can decide whether to create your own soapy solution or buy a bottle of bubbles from the store. If you have more than one kid, ask one to be the blower and the other one to be the bubble popper. Create a competition of who can pop the most bubbles under a minute. Another fun competition is seeing who can blow the largest bubble.

9. Water Balloon Dodgeball

What better way to motivate your children to play outside than to fill some balloons with water and allow them to toss the balloons at each other? There are many fun games you can play with water balloons; one of them is dodgeball. The aim of dodgeball is to avoid getting hit by a flying ball, while attempting to get the opposing players out by hitting them with a ball. The game ends when one team's players have all been sent out.

10. Egg and Spoon Race

Create an obstacle course in your garden by laying down pieces of wood, tape, or any other type of marker. To win the game, your child must complete the obstacle course without dropping the egg balancing on a spoon. Create more of a challenge by setting a timer and encouraging your child to finish the course before the time runs up!

Coloring Break

Chapter 4:

Unleash Your Creativity

"Too often we give children answers to remember rather than problems to solve."

–Roger Lewin

Creativity With ADHD

One of the most common complaints amongst children with ADHD is boredom. Since they crave constant mental stimulation, they can get easily bored with routines. This often means that to keep your child happy, you need to keep tasks feeling new and interesting. Creativity is the golden thread that can keep your novelty-seeking child engaged, relaxed, and feeling positive. It offers them an outlet to release energy, solve problems, and explore abstract ideas. The following creative activities will not only pique your child's interest, they will also have them preoccupied for hours!

Creative Activities to Activate Your Child's Imagination

A child with ADHD who doesn't get a lot of creative free time is like a fizzy soda bottle that is shaken and ready to burst! When your child isn't directed toward activities where their mind can run wild, they will soon become restless and irritable. If you are looking for new and unexpected ways to spend free time, the following 10 activities have you covered!

1. Finger Painting Collage

Before you open the paint, lay down large sheets of paper on a flat table to protect the furniture. Take another large sheet and place it in front of your child. Using a paintbrush, have them add strokes of paint on the palm of their left or right hand. If they are young, assist them in placing their hand flat and still on the paper before quickly lifting it up. Continue to make handprints on the paper until most of the white space has been filled with colorful hands. Don't forget to bring a bowl of soapy water so your child can wash off and reapply different colored paints.

2. Doodling

Younger children find doodling on paper relaxing and mentally stimulating. Take out a few different craft supplies, such as crayons, markers, glitter, feathers, and glue. Lay them out in front of your child and ask them to draw whatever comes to mind. If there is a family member's birthday coming up, or perhaps a popular public holiday, use it as inspiration for the drawing.

3. Pretend Play

Role-playing gives you and your child a great excuse to dress up and spend an hour or so in an imaginary world. To make the most out of role-playing, make sure you have plenty of props, recycled materials, costumes, and any other interesting items that your child can play with. You will also need to create a scenario that spurs your child's imagination. Some common scenarios include:

- Sick patient visiting doctor's office.

- Mother or father taking care of their child.

- Grocery shopping and hosting a tea party.

- Having a conversation on the phone.

- Teacher giving a lesson in front of students.

Don't miss out on the opportunity to turn pretend play into a teachable moment. You can ask your child for insight on what they think about certain matters or reiterate the importance of certain values or beliefs, such as treating others how you would like to be treated.

4. Create a Storybook

Take four A4 (8x11-½ inches) cardboard pieces of paper. Stack them horizontally and fold in half. Flatten the cardboard to make a solid and defined crease. Open them and punch three or four staples along the crease. Now you have your mini book ready!

The next part involves creative writing—or making a collage of pictures if you have a small child. If your child has never created a story before, they will need your help coming up with a plot line and creating a few characters. To make things easier, you can ask your child to create a story based on your family or their friends.

If your child is young, have them tell the story to you while you write it out on each page. An older child may want to write out the story on their own. The remainder of the time can be spent cutting out photos from a magazine, adding stickers, and decorating the book with various craft supplies together.

5. Salt Painting

On a paper or plastic plate, pour half a cup of Epsom salt. If you like, you can bunch the salt in four different areas on the plate to create different colors. Bring out a variety of food coloring from the kitchen and pour a few drops on the salt, mixing with a disposable teaspoon.

Next, ask your child to doodle on medium-sized cardboard paper. The shapes or patterns must be big enough to fill with the salt mixture. Alternatively, you can use a stencil of your child's favorite animal or cartoon. When you are ready, apply craft glue to the areas of the picture where you want to add salt. Let your child pour the salt over the areas, and then give it an hour to dry.

6. Taking Turns Creating Art

Creating art can be an awesome way to bond with your child! Go outside with a few craft supplies and a medium-sized piece of paper. Take the lead by drawing an unusual image or pattern on the paper, and then pass the paper to your child. It is now their turn to add to the picture by drawing an unusual image or pattern. Continue passing the paper back and forth until you both are satisfied with your masterpiece.

7. Marble Painting

What kid doesn't enjoy playing with marbles? A marble painting is a creative way of taking one of your child's favorite toys and finding an interesting way to play with them. All you will need is a medium-sized piece of cardboard paper, various paint colors, and marbles. Have your child dip a marble in paint and roll it over the paper. Supervise the activity, and when they are done, wash the marbles and leave the paper to dry for an hour.

8. Shaving Cream Playdough

Your child may already have shop-bought playdough of their own. But wouldn't it be fun if they could make their own—with Dad's shaving cream? This activity is simple to carry out, and it will only require three ingredients: food coloring, ½ cup of corn starch, and ½ cup of shaving cream.

Combine the starch, shaving cream, and food coloring in a bowl. Knead the ingredients together until it starts to take shape. Feel free to let your child have a go at kneading the dough, too! The crumbly mixture will eventually start to take on a dough-like consistency. When you are satisfied with the shape, you can hand it over to your child to mold into various shapes and characters.

9. Create Face Masks

You can take pretend play up a level by creating unique masks. To create your own masks, you will need a paper plate, scissors, black marker, craft supplies, glue, and rubber bands.

The first step is to take a black marker and outline shapes for the eyes, nose, and mouth. Use scissors to cut out the shapes, leaving eye-like, nose-like, and mouth-like holes (if your child is old enough, let them do the cutting).

The next step is to decorate the mask using various craft supplies. If your child desires to recreate a specific animal or superhero, help them choose the right colors to bring their mask to life.

The final step is to punch two holes on the left and right side of the plate (typically where the ears would be). Take rubber bands and tie them on each side, leaving a big enough loop for your child to fit around their ears.

10. Fruit Cubes

Get creative with your summertime beverages by making fruit cubes with your child. The recipe is as easy as selecting colorful fruits, placing them inside an ice cube tray, and allowing them to freeze for at least four hours. Pop the cubes out of the tray and serve them with water, fruit juice, or lemonade!

Coloring Break

Chapter 5:

Step Into the Kitchen

"The kitchen really is the castle itself. This is where we spend our happiest moments and where we find the joy of being a family."

–Mario Batali

A Recipe for Success

Research shows that consuming the right diet can reduce symptoms of ADHD in children. However, as you may know, these children tend to be fussy eaters! One of the best ways to expose your child to healthy foods and get them excited about mealtime is to enjoy preparing meals with them. Teaching your child how to prepare simple dishes will provide them with a rich sensory experience, improve their organizational skills, and cause them to have a positive relationship with food. The following 10 recipes offer your child a sensory building activity to enjoy!

Super Easy Kid-Friendly Recipes

Children born in this technological age are growing up in a world where nearly everything is automated, processed, delivered, and offered with uttermost convenience. This means that they are missing out on learning some of the basic skills, such as cooking. It is important for your child to understand what food they are eating, where it comes from, and how it is prepared, so they can feel empowered to take care of their growing bodies. Below are 10 quirky recipes to prepare with your child in the kitchen.

1. Banana Sushi

Banana sushi is *not* fruit wrapped in seaweed. It is chunks of banana rolled in candy and other sweet and savory spreads of your choice. These yummy treats are best served as lunchtime snacks or fun party treats. What's more, bananas are a rich source of vitamin B6 and potassium, which are excellent for children with ADHD.

Ingredients

- 2-4 bananas
- Cinnamon sugar
- 2-4 spoons of almond butter
- Crushed cereal
- Ground coconut
- 2-4 spoons of whipped cream cheese
- Chocolate sprinkles

Directions

- Peel a banana and cut it into 1-1/2 inch (3 cm) pieces.
- Roll the banana in either almond butter or whipped cream cheese.
- Cover the banana in your favorite sweet or savory coating.
- Leave on a tray to set and roll the next piece.

Total time: 5 minutes

2. Strawberry-Peanut Butter Wraps

If you are looking for a tasty lunchbox snack, why not make delicious strawberry-peanut butter wraps? Peanut butter is a great source of plant-based protein for growing kids. If your child has nut allergies, you can replace peanut butter with sunflower seed butter.

Ingredients

- 4-6 spoons of peanut butter (or any alternative)
- 2 tortilla wraps
- 10 medium to large strawberries, thinly sliced

Directions

- Place tortilla wraps on two plates and spread 2-3 spoons of peanut butter over them.

- Divide the strawberries equally between both wraps, placing them along the middle.

- Tightly roll each wrap and seal the edges with peanut butter.

- Cut the wrap into bite-sized pieces (1-1/2 inches or 3 cm) and serve!

Total time: 2 minutes

3. Whole Wheat Pizza Bagels

Ditch the frozen pizzas and make your own healthy whole wheat pizza bagels. These yummy meals are suitable for children who have just started eating solid foods. After baking them in the oven, they come out soft and covered in melted cheese and warm tomato sauce. Delicious!

Ingredients

- ½ cup tomato sauce

- ¼ teaspoon dry herbs

- ¼ garlic powder

- 6 mini whole wheat bagels, cut in half

- ¾ cup grated mozzarella cheese

Directions

- Preheat the oven to 425 degrees Fahrenheit (180 degrees Celsius).

- Add the tomato sauce and herbs into a bowl; stir together.

- Place bagel halves on a baking sheet and spread tomato mixture on each one.

- Finish off by sprinkling mozzarella cheese on each bagel

- Bake for 10 minutes.

- Leave to cool before serving.

Total time: 11 minutes

4. Pizza Hot Dogs

Traditional hot dogs are tasty, but when your child gets bored with the same old hot dog-and-bun combo, you can switch it up and use pizza dough instead. The best part about biting into the crunchy golden dough is discovering a gooey cheesy and meaty center inside. Your child is guaranteed to enjoy every mouthful!

Ingredients

- 6 meat or vegetarian hot dogs

- ½ cup tomato sauce

- 1 pound whole wheat pizza dough (at room temperature)

- 3 pieces of string cheese

Direction

- Preheat the oven to 425 degrees Fahrenheit (180 degrees Celsius).

- Break the dough into six round balls.

- Roll each piece of dough into a long rope, about four times the length of a normal hot dog.

- Slice each string cheese in half lengthwise.

- Slice each hot dog in half, but make sure your knife doesn't reach the ends.

- Place one stick of cheese inside a hot dog. Do this for all six hot dogs.

- Start from one end of the hot dog and wrap the dough around until you reach the other end.

- Once all hot dogs have been wrapped in dough, place them on a greased baking sheet.

- Bake for 15-18 minutes, or until the dough looks golden brown.

Total time: 25–30 minutes

5. Mixed Berry Oatmeal Smoothie

Have you run out of healthy breakfast options? The whole family is bound to love this easy smoothie recipe! Oatmeal is another excellent source of protein and complex carbohydrates, which ensures that your child's body releases energy sustainably throughout the day—and focuses better at school!

Ingredients

- 1 cup unsweetened almond milk.

- 1 teaspoon maple syrup

- 1 banana

- ½ teaspoon ground cinnamon

- 1 cup frozen mixed berries

- ¼ cup instant oatmeal

- Pinch of sea salt

Directions

- Place the first six ingredients inside a blender and process them until you achieve a smooth consistency.

- Pour the drink over ice and sprinkle it with a pinch of sea salt. Serve immediately.

Total time: 5 minutes

6. Breakfast Parfait

This delicious combination of granola, fruit, and yogurt is easy to prepare with your child. Plus, they can choose different types of fruits to add each time you make them. Similar to oatmeal, granola is high in protein and fiber, making it a great breakfast option!

Ingredients

- 4 cups vanilla yogurt

- 2 spoons honey

- 2 medium apples, sliced

- 2 cups fresh blackberries

- ½ cup granola (without raisins)

Directions

- Use a kid-friendly small or medium mug or cup.

- Layer yogurt, granola, honey, apple slices, and blackberries.
- Create another layer with the same ingredients until the cup is full.

Total time: 10 minutes

7. Chicken Ranch Wraps

If you have some leftover chicken from the night before, this recipe is guaranteed to impress your child! The combination of a salad, meat, and flavorful dressing can be a great way to introduce your child to new vegetables, too (without getting into a brawl). If you are concerned with the nutritional value of the dressing, go for a low-fat or fat-free option.

Ingredients

- 1 cup cooked, shredded chicken
- 1 cup shredded lettuce (you can use spinach or kale as a substitute)
- 4 flour tortilla wraps
- 1 large tomato, sliced
- 1 medium green or yellow pepper, sliced
- 1 cup grated cheddar cheese
- ⅓ cup ranch salad dressing

Directions

- Place tortilla wrap on a plate.
- Layer lettuce, chicken, tomato, peppers, and cheese.
- Drizzle salad dressing.
- Roll the wrap tightly and cut in half or thirds.

Total time: 10 minutes

8. Garlic Bread Pizza Sandwiches

If you are tired of making grilled cheese sandwiches, spice things up by making pizza sandwiches. The main difference from a traditional cheese sandwich is, of course, the pizza toppings, which also give your child an opportunity to use their imagination and come up with all sorts of variations!

Ingredients

- 1 pack of frozen garlic Texas toast
- Pepperoni slices
- Mushroom slices
- ¼ cup pasta sauce
- Cheese slices

Directions

- Preheat sandwich griller on low to medium heat.
- Add the garlic toast and cook until both sides are golden brown (3 minutes on each side of the toast).
- Open the griller and add a spoonful of pasta sauce. Top with the remaining ingredients. Close the sandwich and allow the bread to grill for another 3 minutes, or until the cheese has melted.
- Take the sandwich off the griller and serve. If you like, you can add another spoonful of sauce over the sandwich for added flavor.

Total time: 20 minutes

9. Peach Yogurt Swirls

Have you noticed we have included many recipes with fruit? This is because research shows that fresh fruits and vegetables can reduce inattention in children with ADHD. This final fruit recipe is great as a hot summer's day snack.

Ingredients

- 4 paper or plastic cups
- ¼ cup cold water
- 2 tablespoons sugar
- 2-¾ cups fat-free honey Greek yogurt
- 1 cup peaches, diced
- 4 wooden pop sticks

Directions

- Take a cup and fill it with ¼ cup of yogurt.

- Blend water, sugar, and peaches in a food processor until the peaches are finely chopped.

- Put 1-½ tablespoons of the peach mixture into each cup.

- Gently stir the fruit into the yogurt to create a swirl.

- Cover the cup with foil and insert a pop stick through the foil before placing the cup in the freezer.

- Repeat the same instructions for the other three cups. Leave the cups inside the freezer for a day.

Total time: 15 minutes

10. Gooey Cheese Fries

Cheese fries are not the healthiest meal to serve your child, but every once in a while, they can be a great treat! What's great about this recipe is the level of convenience. Frozen fry packets can be refrigerated and reheated, which means that you can get food on the table a lot quicker. Other than that, this meal is all about pure indulgence!

Ingredients

- 1 packet frozen steak fries

- ½ teaspoon garlic powder

- ¼ teaspoon onion powder

- Pinch of paprika

- 1 can condensed cheddar cheese soup (undiluted)

- ¼ cup 2% milk

Directions

- Grease an oven tray and spread around frozen steak fries.

- Bake the fries at 450 degrees Fahrenheit (180 degrees Celsius), or until they look crispy and golden.

- While your fries are baking, heat soup, milk, garlic powder, and onion powder in a saucepan.

- Take the fries out of the oven and arrange them in bowls or plates. Drizzle the creamy soup mixture over the fries and add a sprinkle of paprika.

Total time: 20 minutes

For extra precaution and order in the kitchen, plan ahead of time which cooking tasks you would like your child to help with. Read over the recipe with them and explain what they will be doing. Always make sure that your child stays away from sharp kitchen objects and open flames. Give them an apron and other safety gear to keep them safe and ensure maximum enjoyment!

Coloring Break

Chapter 6:

Think Like Einstein

"Children learn as they play. Most importantly, in play children learn how to learn."

–O. Fred Donaldson

Helping Your Kid Become a Problem Solver

Similar to adults, children run into challenges, too. Sure, their challenges may look different, but it is still beneficial for children to develop problem-solving skills. One of the common symptoms of ADHD is executive dysfunction, which affects a child's ability to think critically. To enhance problem-solving skills, it is important to play games that develop this important life skill, which over time will make them more confident in tackling challenges. The following fun activities will teach your child how to become a better problem solver.

Problem-Solving Activities to Nourish Your Child's Mind

Teaching your child to solve problems began when they were a toddler, crawling to fetch a bottle or toy placed a few feet away. As they grew up, they learned how to solve more personal problems, like how to brush their teeth and tie their shoe laces. In a few years, when your child reaches adolescence, they will be given more responsibility and encouraged to solve more complex problems. Therefore, reinforcing problem-solving skills is something you will need to continuously do as your child grows. Below are fantastic mind-stimulating activities you can complete with your child.

1. Marble Maze

Spatial learning is the ability to observe, analyze, and understand your environment. Marble maze encourages your child to create a mental representation of their environment by figuring out how to move a marble from one point to another on a piece of paper.

Before the game begins, draw a maze on a piece of paper with a black marker. Clearly mark the start and end points. Ask your child to grab a few marbles and position them at the starting point. The goal is to move each marble through the maze until it reaches the end. An older child is not allowed to touch the marble. They are supposed to tilt the piece of paper in different directions to guide the marble across the maze.

2. Block Tower

Building any kind of object helps your child learn about gravity and structure. You can use a variety of building materials to construct a tower, such as construction blocks, toilet paper rolls, or any other sturdy object. The challenge is to create a tower that can balance without falling over. To increase the challenge, set a timer or encourage your child to build the tower using unusual objects.

3. Play Puzzles

Puzzles are a fun activity for kids of all ages. Based on your child's age, you can select a puzzle that provides a challenge, but that can be completed within a reasonable time. Completing puzzles can improve the way your child analyzes problems and troubleshoots to find the best solution.

4. Impromptu Acting

Divide the family into teams. Take a piece of paper and pen, and write down different real-life scenarios, such as playing basketball or watching a movie. Fold the pieces of paper and place them inside a bowl.

Each team picks a scenario and acts it out without talking. The other team is supposed to guess what the scenario is. If they guess right, it is their turn to pick a scenario and act it out. If they cannot guess it, the team doing the acting gets to play again. These kinds of impromptu activities help children identify problems, formulate solutions, and execute them.

5. Survival Scenario Cards

Create medium-sized cards with unique survival scenarios, such as being deserted on an island, only having one number to call, or being home alone. Read out each card to your child and ask them to share what they would do under those circumstances. You can give them 5 minutes to think about how they would solve the problem.

6. Egg Drop Challenge

This activity is straightforward: Create a solution to protect an egg from cracking after being dropped from height. There are no restrictions to the kinds of materials your child can use to protect the egg. The goal is for them to go through the process of trial and error, until they can drop an egg without cracking. Make sure that you have enough eggs for your child to use for demonstrations!

7. Guess Who?

This fun guessing game encourages problem-solving and critical thinking. Start off by thinking of a public figure, fictional character, animal, or profession that your child is familiar with. Next, look around the house for three to five clues that are associated with the answer. For instance, if the answer is a dog, you might collect dog food, a collar, a dog picture from the internet, and a dog bed. Give your child an opportunity to guess the answer based on the clues you have provided.

8. Balloon Popping Challenge

Every kid loves popping balloons as much as they love playing with them. For this challenge, ask your child to go around the house looking for different materials to pop a balloon without using their hands. The only materials not permitted are sharp objects, like building tools, kitchen knives, and any other unsafe object. To moderate the materials, you can select five to 10 materials that your kid can experiment with.

9. Build an Identical Block

Instead of letting your child build their own tower, create a model out of building blocks and challenge them to build an identical one. Make sure you give them the same number and shapes of blocks that were used to build your model. Depending on their age, you can make the model as simple or complex as required. Offer hints every now and again, but otherwise allow them to do most of the critical thinking themselves.

10. Scavenger Hunt

This activity is great for developing problem-solving skills because it encourages your child to think out of the box. Create an objective for the hunt, such as finding a missing item around the house. Hide clues in different locations that guide your child to the item. Write each clue using simple language to ensure your child knows where to go next. It might also help to make the clues large and colorful enough to find when they reach each location (i.e., having large yellow envelopes, semi-visible, in various areas of the house).

Coloring Break

Chapter 7:

Explore the City

"There are no seven wonders of the world in the eyes of a child. There are seven million."

–Walt Streightiff

Creating Memories, One Experience at a Time

A child is naturally curious and enjoys learning and exploring new fascinations. There is only so much stimulation your child can get at home before they get bored. At times, the best way to satisfy your child's insatiable curiosity is to leave the house for a day and visit places nearby. The following suggestions will help you organize the next family day trip or mini vacation.

Fun Places to Visit With Your Child

Have you ever considered how exploring the world with your child develops their self-confidence? Every time you go out, they are exposed to different people, cultures, and lifestyles, which increases their social awareness, empathy, and willingness to venture outside of their comfort zone.

One day, your child will leave the comfort of home and explore the world on their own. You can rest assured that all of the small trips they took as a child will be enough preparation to live an enriching and independent life! The following travel places are kid-friendly and suitable for the whole family to enjoy!

1. Theme Parks

Theme parks offer a full day's worth of rides, shows, and games for the entire family. It is important to manage your child's expectations before arriving at the park. For example, you may want to explain that certain rides are only for children who are a certain age, and therefore they may not be able to go on every ride in the park. It is also important to prepare your child for the walking and long queues. To avoid crowds of people and sensory overload, it is better to visit a theme park during off-peak days or weeks.

2. Kid-Friendly Resorts and Cruises

Resorts and cruises are a great option when you are looking for vacation spots that provide access to fun activities. Kid-friendly activities may include large swimming pools, resort theme parks, hiking trails, water sports, camping, or kids' social clubs. When researching vacation spots, consider what kinds of activities your child loves to do and find places that match those interests.

3. National Parks

If you are the type of family that enjoys the great outdoors, you may love visiting a national park. There are plenty of outdoor activities available throughout parks nationwide, such as fishing, kayaking, hiking, or camping. Make sure that you pack a reading book, puzzles, and toys for your child to play with during downtime or when the weather isn't looking good.

4. Local Zoos and Aquariums

Local zoo and aquarium visits teach your child about animal behavior and help them cultivate empathy. They might get to see the animals feeding, sleeping, or playing with each other. Having such close contact with animals can also increase your child's awareness of the environment and learn how to interact with different animals.

5. Museums

Museums can be a fun excursion for children of all ages, but more especially for children with ADHD. They offer a chance to learn about world history, different people, and cultures across the globe. What makes museums suitable for children with ADHD is that although their minds are being stimulated, the environment is not overwhelming. You can even select which type of museum you would like to visit based on your child's current interests.

6. Beaches and Lakes

Another fun family outing is a trip to the beach or lake. This activity is suitable for families who enjoy being around water and participating in water activities. There are a lot of activities you can enjoy at the beach, such as building sand castles, swimming, pretend play, or playing beach volleyball. If you have older kids, search for a beach resort or vacation spot that offers a variety of age-appropriate water sports, like surfing or water skiing. Some beach facilities may even offer surfing school or safety lessons before going into the water.

7. Local Farm or Ranch

Younger children will enjoy spending the day on a farm or ranch, where they get to learn about how crops are grown, livestock is tended, and various food products that are packaged there, like milk or cheese. Other activities that are offered on farms and ranches are horse or pony riding, petting and feeding animals, as well as picking fruits and vegetables.

8. Visiting Cities

Take a trip to a nearby city with rich history and culture. Your child will enjoy sight-seeing, trying out new foods, visiting museums and other historical landmarks, and other kid-friendly attractions. To avoid crowds, visit during off-peak seasons and limit the amount of time you spend at one attraction. In general, smaller, tourist-friendly cities tend to be less busy throughout the year than larger commercial cities.

9. Ski Resorts

If you are not afraid of cold weather, why not visit a ski resort? It can be a great opportunity for the whole family to learn how to ski on mountainous slopes or enjoy other activities, like ice skating, snow tubing, or indoor craft-making (when you would much prefer staying inside). Look for ski resorts with plenty of kid-friendly activities—and an option to get a licensed guide to assist you.

10. Camping

Taking your child camping can offer a sensory experience of a lifetime. They can breathe in the fresh air, fall asleep to the sounds of crickets, eat food prepared on the fire, and get their hands dirty. Older kids may learn a few survival skills from camping, such as making a campfire, setting up a tent, or purifying drinking water. They will also gain confidence by solving problems and learning how to handle themselves in uncommon environments.

Coloring Break

Chapter 8:

Take a Moment to Breathe

"Happiness can always be found, even in the darkest of times, if only one remembers to turn on the light."

–Dumbledore

When Excitement Turns to Restlessness

One of the hallmark symptoms of ADHD is overstimulation. Your child might be enjoying a trip to the mall, and then suddenly show signs of distress. This almost immediate switch occurs due to their inability to process a lot of different stimuli at one time. An otherwise pleasurable experience can quickly turn frustrating, and neither you nor your child can enjoy the outing. When your child is emotionally triggered, you can turn to one of the following coping strategies to help them calm down and feel balanced again.

Effective Stress-Busting Activities to Calm Your Kid

Stress is often seen as a condition affecting mostly adults. However, children born in this modern age are also exposed to the pressures of living in a fast-paced environment, such as juggling school demands, household chores, family relationships, and extracurricular activities. Teaching your child how to manage stress in positive ways can increase their resilience during difficult times. Below are simple stress-busting activities to help your child calm down.

1. Mindful Breathing

When your child slows down their breathing and takes deeper breaths, it can instantly induce a state of relaxation. A technique known as mindful breathing can help your child shift their focus from the stressful event to their breathing pattern. Ask your child to close their eyes and inhale through their nose. As they do, count up to four slowly. Tell them to release the breath out of their mouth slowly.

guiding them for another four counts. Repeat this pattern until they are feeling more emotionally stable.

2. Tap Into the Senses

One way to reverse overstimulation is to slow things down. This means focusing on one stimulus at a time. Take your child into a room and play a sensory exercise. Go through each of the five senses—sight, touch, smell, hearing, and taste—and ask them to identify as many items as they can in the room. For example, you can ask them to identify five things they can see, four things they can touch, three things they can smell, and so on.

3. Count Up to 10 Together

Counting is another great exercise that can minimize anxiety and distract your child from negative thinking. Whenever you sense that they are feeling worried, sit on a couch together, facing each other, and both of you start slowly counting to 10. When you get to 10, count backward until you get back to one.

4. Writing Prompts Journaling

When your child is proficient in writing, you could introduce them to journaling. Think of it as a therapeutic exercise to transfer big thoughts and emotions to paper. What's great is your child doesn't need to have creative writing skills to start journaling. They can use writing prompts as inspiration to share how they are feeling.

5. Blindfolded Taste Test

Another sensory exercise to reduce stress is blindfold your child and ask them to smell, touch, and taste food on a teaspoon to figure out what it is. You can make this exercise as easy or difficult as you like by presenting your child with some of their favorite foods, along with others they have never tasted before. Have a glass of water and empty bowl nearby in case your child wants to spit out the food.

6. Positive Affirmation Jar

Find an empty jar and lid in the house. Decorate the jar with your child by wrapping it in paper, adding glitter, or painting it. When you are done decorating the jar, you shouldn't be able to see what is inside. Next, take small pieces of colorful note paper and ask your child to offer you suggestions of positive statements. These should be statements that resonate with them and feel encouraging. Write each statement on a note, fold the paper, and place it inside the jar. Close the jar and hand it over to your child to keep in their room. Whenever they need a pick-me-up, remind them of their jar. They can select a note for affirmation.

7. Straw Painting

Art is a fantastic form of therapy that can induce a feeling of relaxation. An interesting type of art that incorporates deep breathing is straw painting. The aim is to spread watered-down watercolor paint across a medium-sized cardboard paper, using a drinking straw. Each deep breath directs the paint in different directions on the paper, creating an interesting piece of art.

8. Guided Meditation

There are plenty of kid-friendly guided meditation videos online. The purpose of guided meditation is to help your child pay attention to what they are feeling without reacting. When you sense that your child is overwhelmed, encourage them to follow along with a guided meditation script. Some popular YouTube channels that offer guided meditations are the Meditation Channel, Peace Out, and Cosmic Kids.

9. Make a Stress Ball

Stress balls present a positive way to relieve stress and anxiety at home or at school. Even though you can easily buy one online, it can be more fun helping your child make their own. All you need to make a stress ball are balloons, a funnel, and flour. Use the funnel to fill the uninflated balloon with flour. You can decide how big you want your ball to be; however, it should be big enough to fit in your child's hands. Tie the balloon, then place it inside another balloon (just in case the pressure makes the first balloon tear).

10. Coloring

Coloring pictures is an activity for children of all ages—and even adults! Similar to painting or other forms of art, coloring can be a positive distraction to stop overthinking and other anxiety-causing thoughts. You can look for coloring books suitable for your child's age and preferences. There are a few coloring pictures included throughout this workbook that your child can enjoy, too!

Coloring Break

Chapter 9:

Get Talking

"There's a lot of talk these days about giving children self-esteem. It's not something you can give; it's something they have to build."

—Randy Pausch

Teaching Your Child to Be an Effective Communicator

Children with ADHD tend to have trouble sharing their thoughts and feelings effectively. Some of the typical communication issues they might experience are blurting information without thinking about it, struggling to follow instructions, talking excessively, or interrupting others when they are speaking. Since building relationships is an essential part of your growing child's life, it is important for them to develop strong communication skills. The following activities offer fun ways to teach your child how to process and interpret information and come up with a considered response.

Activities to Improve Your Child's Communication Skills

Did you know that one of the best ways to improve your child's communication skills is to talk to them a lot? You might be thinking, "I don't have that problem because my child never stops talking!" But how much of what they say reinforces good communication techniques? As a parent, you can step in and teach them new vocabulary, comprehension and memory skills, how to describe what they are feeling, and other skills that will improve their communication. The following activities provide fun ways to develop communication skills.

1. Guess the Object

Take an empty shoe box and seal it shut with tape. Cut a hole on the side, big enough to insert a small object and for your child to fit their hand. Find an object with an interesting texture and place it inside the box. Ask your child to feel the object without peeking inside. The aim of the game is to get them to describe the object in many different ways before eventually pulling it out.

2. Songwriting Challenge

Challenge your child to write a song from scratch. They can decide on the topic and how long the song should be, as well as what kind of up-tempo backing track they would like to use (you can find free music samples online). This challenge can have many parts, such as writing the lyrics on paper, getting Mom or Dad to approve, then practicing singing the lyrics over the melody. At the end, you can bring the family together to watch your child's musical performance.

3. Create an Emotions Wheel

It can be frustrating for your child to sense strong emotions without the vocabulary to express how they are feeling. An emotions wheel is a great way to introduce young children to basic emotions and teach them how to identify what they are feeling, especially during an emotional outburst when they cannot think objectively.

To create an emotions wheel, take an A3 (11-3/4 x 16-1/2 inch) piece of cardboard paper and trace a big circle. Use scissors to cut out the circle (they can help if they're old enough to cut safely). Using a pencil or marker, divide the circle into 10 equal triangles. Each triangle should include a label for an emotion. Below are 10 emotions your child may experience:

- Calm

- Worried

- Surprised

- Scared

- Embarrassed

- Sad

- Happy

- Confused

- Angry

- Bored

You can also include a picture representing each emotion (either draw the picture yourself or find an emoji from the internet). If you like, you can add a light spinning object at the center of the wheel. Here is an example of a wheel created by Mentally Healthy Schools. Talk to your child about the emotion they are feeling and help them describe it. If they are too young to describe it, ask them to draw their own visual representation of the emotion.

4. Pass the Mic

Taking turns when speaking is a sign of politeness. You can teach your child how to patiently allow others to speak without interrupting them by playing a game of pass the mic. Essentially, the "mic" can be any object you have in the house, such as a toy, wooden spoon, or piece of rolled-up stationery.

Create a list of topics that you can discuss with your child. Ask them to sit down, and then place the mic between the two of you. Tell them that the only time someone can speak is when they are holding the mic. Grab the mic and begin the conversation. When you have said all you want to say, place the mic down and gesture for your child to pick it up. While they are speaking, silently nod or smile, but avoid making a sound. Hold them to the same standards when you are speaking.

5. Interpreting Photos

Grab a few different types of magazines and go through them with your child. When you get to an interesting picture of people performing an action, or displaying some type of emotion, stop and ask your child what is happening in the photo. Give them some time to process the visual information and come to a conclusion. There are no right or wrong answers since you are encouraging your child to come up with detailed responses.

6. Broken Telephone

Broken telephone is a fun game that requires participation from the whole family. The objective is to see how far a message can travel from one person to another without being distorted.

Instruct your family to sit in a circle or around a table. Have one person start the game by whispering a word, phrase, or sentence in another person's ear. The message is then whispered to the person sitting on the left or right, and so on, until the last person in the circle or table blurts out what they heard. The person who started the game will compare the final message to their original message.

7. Guess the Emotion

Another game suitable for families is "Guess the Emotion." Write down a list of emotions on a stack of blank cards (feel free to add a visual aid). Put the stack of cards upside down (hiding the labels) on a table. Each family member takes a turn picking a card and acting out the emotion for others to guess. For example, if the card says "Angry," they can pretend to yell at someone. The person who guesses correctly wins that round.

8. Follow the Instructions

Create a list of instructions to perform a household chore, such as making the bed, washing dishes, or picking up dirty clothes and putting them in the washing machine. Make sure the task is age-appropriate and doesn't involve too many steps.

Write down the instructions on a piece of paper, offering as much guidance as possible. You can even include illustrations, colors, or diagrams to make it easier for your child to follow. The last instruction should be "Write down your name on the top of this paper and return it to Mommy/Daddy." Check to see how many instructions your child was able to follow.

9. Copycat

While it is important for your child to learn verbal communication skills, it is just as important for them to know how to read nonverbal cues. Copycat is a fun game that is guaranteed to bring a lot of laughter. To begin, sit down on a couch facing your child. Encourage them to maintain eye contact with you. Act out various facial expressions or body gestures, and then have your child repeat them after you. No talking is allowed during this game since the aim is to increase awareness of body language.

10. Back-and-Forth Storytelling

This game can be played in a small or large group (the more people, the better the outcome). One person begins by starting the story. A common phrase would be "Once upon a time there was ..." Moving either from left or right, each person takes a turn to offer a sentence that adds onto the story. The quirkier and more original the sentences are, the funnier the story! Continue to go around the circle, adding to the story until one person wraps it up by saying, "And they lived happily ever after."

Coloring Break

Chapter 10:

Sleep Peacefully

"I find that most parents who do not have a formal bedtime routine typically spend that last hour before bed fighting with their children about going to bed."

–Elizabeth Pantley

ADHD and Sleep Problems

As much as 70% of children with ADHD experience sleep problems (Sciberras, 2020). These may range from bedtime anxiety and having difficulty sleeping to resisting going to bed and only being able to sleep under certain conditions (e.g., after watching a specific show on TV). There are various interventions you can try to improve your child's quality of sleep. The following activities are designed to get your child into a relaxing bedtime routine and help them go to bed feeling sleepy.

Activities to End the Bedtime Struggle

A bedtime routine consists of a set of rituals that are performed in the same order every night to prepare you for bedtime. They are strategically chosen to burn energy and calm your mind. Putting your child on a bedtime routine can improve their natural sleeping patterns and train their brain to anticipate sleep time.

Studies have shown that bedtime routines can also improve your child's memory and positively influence their mental health. The following activities are designed to burn as much extra energy as possible before your child goes to bed. If you like, you can incorporate them as part of your child's bedtime routine.

1. Monkey Tails

The game of Monkey Tails is similar to the game of tag. The only difference is that players run around with a sock or piece of fabric tucked in their pants, which must be retrieved in order for them to be sent out. The last player who still has their tail intact wins the game!

2. Marco Polo

Why not take a dip in the pool before showering and getting ready for bed? A classic pool game that your child will certainly love is known as Marco Polo. This game is another variation of tag. One player swims around the pool with their eyes shut, yelling "Marco!" The other players are supposed to reply, "Polo!" and attempt to get away from the player without getting caught. The first player to be caught starts the game off again.

3. Red Light, Green Light

This classic game is designed to get your child running! Go out into the garden and create start and finish lines. Position your child at the starting line and tell them to wait for your instructions. When you say, "Green light," they are supposed to run toward the finish line, and stop as soon as you say, "Red light," Make sure that you create a few stop-and-starts throughout the game to tire out your child. For older kids, you can include a "yellow light," which means hopping on one foot.

4. Do Some Stretching

Stretching is a relaxing, low-intensity exercise that relieves tension from the body. You can soothe your child before bed by leading them through a few kid-friendly stretches. Play some calming music in the background, dim the lights, and burn a candle to enhance the ambience.

5. Dance Battle

There are more ways to move your body before bed, like challenging your child to a dance battle! Move the furniture out of the way and create a dance floor in your living room. Invite your child to show you some of their best dance moves, and then show them some of your own. The weirder the dance moves, the better!

6. Simon Says

Play a few rounds of Simon Says and encourage your child to follow everything you do. Start off with basic instructions, like touching their nose or toes. Once you have their attention, lead them in basic stretches or yoga poses. Finally, when it is time for bedtime, let the final command be "Simon says go to bed."

7. Go on a Treasure Hunt

Hide five to 10 of your child's bedtime essentials in various locations around the house. For instance, you could hide their pajamas, toothbrush, reading book, and their favorite stuffed animal. The goal is to find all of the items and complete the bedtime routine (i.e., brush their teeth after finding the toothbrush) before eventually heading off to bed.

8. Early Lights Out

Too much light coming from ceiling lights or electronic devices can interfere with the body's natural sleep rhythm. You can prepare your child for bedtime by switching off the lights around the house early. Strategically place lamps around the house so everybody can see where they are walking. Enjoy candle-lit dinners and bathtime, and use a flashlight when reading bedtime stories.

9. Stargazing

Being outdoors in the evenings may be invigorating for adults, but it makes young kids feel sleepy. Grab a blanket, pillow, reading book, flashlight, and binoculars, and go out into the garden. Find a spot where you can see the night sky and look for constellations. If stargazing gets boring, take out the reading book and have story time outside before making your way back indoors.

10. Family Bonding Time

Before everyone goes their separate ways, call the family together for some bonding times. Go around the group sharing your highs and lows for the day, things that you are grateful for, and what you are looking forward to. To ensure that there are no interruptions, introduce the mic (refer back to Chapter 9).

Coloring Break

Conclusion

"You can't change who you are, and you shouldn't be asked to."

–Jonathan Mooney

The common behaviors associated with ADHD, such as constantly fidgeting, an inability to sit still, or acting without thinking, are usually seen as disruptive. However, when we accept the fact that children with ADHD are born with more energy than other kids, these same "disruptive" behaviors become opportunities to find different ways of keeping them stimulated.

Keeping your child busy has probably been one of your greatest challenges as a parent. If your child's brain could talk, it would ask for both quality and quantity when presented with experiences. On the one hand, it craves quality—in the form of novelty—because the same games or tasks repeated over and over again become boring. But on the other hand, it wants a lot of different types of stimuli to satisfy the senses.

This workbook has presented you with 100 activities to feed your child's curiosity, increase physical activity, boost brain power, and develop communication skills (just to name a few). Neither you nor your child should be short of options when it comes to selecting the best activities to play indoors and out, independently or as a family. The combination of play and learning will also ensure that every game your child is taught contributes to their overall well-being and encourages them to be a confident young kid!

The takeaway message from this workbook is that you don't need to change your child in order to integrate them into society, teach them valuable life skills, or help them become more responsible. All you need is to spend more time playing with them (or encouraging them to play), so that they are continuously exposed to learning opportunities.

About the Author

Richard Bass is a well-established author with extensive knowledge and background regarding children's disabilities. He has first-hand experience with children and teens who deal with depression and anxiety. Richard also enjoys researching techniques and ideas to better serve students, as well as providing guidance to parents and caregivers on how to understand and lead their children to success.

Richard wants to share his experience, research, and practices through his writing, as it has proven successful to many parents and students. He feels there is a need for parents and others around the child to fully understand the disability or mental health of the child. He hopes that with his writing, people will be more understanding of children going through these issues.

In regards to his qualifications, Richard holds bachelor's and master's degrees in education as well as several certifications, including special education K-12, and educational administration. Whenever he is not working, reading, or writing, he likes to travel with his family to learn about different cultures and to gather ideas from all around about the upbringing of children, especially those with disabilities. He also researches and learns about different educational systems around the world.

Richard participates in several online groups where parents, educators, doctors, and psychologists share their successes with children with disabilities. He also has his own group where further discussion about his books and techniques take place. Apart from his participation in online groups, Richard attends training related to the upbringing of students with disabilities and leads training in this area.

A Message from the Author

If you enjoyed the book and are interested on further updates or just a place to share your thought with other readers or myself, please join my Facebook group by scanning below!

If you would be interested on receiving a FREE Planner for kids PDF version, by signing up you also receive exclusive notifications to when new content is released and will be able to receive it a promotional price. Scan below to sign up!

Scan below to check out my content on You Tube and learn more about Neurodiversity!

References

ADDitude Editors. (2016, November 28). 10 ADHD quotes to save for a bad day. ADDitude. https://www.additudemag.com/slideshows/adhd-quotes-for-a-bad-day/

ADDitude Editors. (2021, December 13). The messy student's guide to order: ADHD organizing tips. ADDitude. https://www.additudemag.com/helping-adhd-students-get-organized-for-school/#:~:text=The%20reason:%20The%20neurological%20process

Admin. (2020, August 7). How outdoor play can help children with ADHD. Arihant Play. https://www.arihantplay.com/how-outdoor-play-can-help-children-with-adhd/#:~:text=Outdoor%20play%20can%20enable%20ADHD

Aliya Khan. (2018, May 4). 15 Fun and exciting creative activities for kids. FirstCry Parenting. https://parenting.firstcry.com/articles/15-best-creative-activities-for-kids/

Armstrong, T. (2018, April 20). Engaging creativity with ADHD. Www.institute4learning.com. https://www.institute4learning.com/2018/04/20/6-ways-to-engage-the-creative-energies-of-kids-diagnosed-with-adhd/

Ashley. (2022, January 5). Cooking with kids quotes. Saving Mealtime. https://savingmealtime.com/cooking-with-kids-quotes/

Bertin, M. (2022, June 15). How ADHD impacts your child's communication skills—and 11 ways to help. ADDitude. https://www.additudemag.com/communication-skills-for-kids-adhd/

Brain Balance. (n.d.). Indoor exercise and movement ideas for children with ADHD. Www.brainbalancecenters.com. https://www.brainbalancecenters.com/blog/indoor-exercise-movement-ideas-children-adhd

Cahn, L., & Higley, A. (2022, May 5). 30 Easy recipes your kids can make all by themselves. Taste of Home; Taste of Home. https://www.tasteofhome.com/collection/easy-recipes-for-kids-to-make-by-themselves/

CHADD. (n.d.). Yoga could benefit children with ADHD. CHADD. https://chadd.org/adhd-weekly/yoga-could-benefit-children-with-adhd/#:~:text=But%20researchers%20in%20several%20studies

Changing Minds. (n.d.). Creative quotes and quotations on children. Creatingminds.org. http://creatingminds.org/quotes/children.htm

Cherry, K. (2022, April 26). 9 Fun activities for kids with ADHD. Verywell Mind. https://www.verywellmind.com/fun-activities-for-kids-with-adhd-5235327#toc-get-moving

Cohen, S. C. L., Harvey, D. J., Shields, R. H., Shields, G. S., Rashedi, R. N., Tancredi, D. J., Angkustsiri, K., Hansen, R. L., & Schweitzer, J. B. (2018). Effects of yoga on attention, impulsivity, and hyperactivity in preschool-aged children with attention-deficit hyperactivity disorder symptoms. Journal of Developmental & Behavioral Pediatrics, 39(3), 200–209. https://doi.org/10.1097/dbp.0000000000000552

Day, N. (2019, July 6). How to help children with ADHD develop problem-solving skills. Raising an Extraordinary Person. https://hes-extraordinary.com/problem-solving-skills-adhd

Dickson, C. (n.d.). How cooking can help children with anxiety. YouthThrive. https://www.youthrive.com.au/articles/how-cooking-can-help-children-with-anxiety/

Dreisbach, S. (2022, September 15). 16 Strength-training exercises for kids. Parents; Parents. https://www.parents.com/fun/sports/exercise/strength-training-exercises-for-kids/

Follows, S. (2022, January 14). Outdoor activities to calm children, how to calm children outdoors. Have Fun Outdoors. https://www.havefunoutdoors.co.uk/outdoor-activities-to-calm-children/

Good Reads. (n.d.-a). A quote from The Last Lecture. Www.goodreads.com. https://www.goodreads.com/quotes/139654-there-s-a-lot-of-talk-these-days-about-giving-children

Good Reads. (n.d.-b). A quote from The No-Cry Sleep Solution. Www.goodreads.com. https://www.goodreads.com/quotes/7507755-until-about-age-ten-or-so-a-child-thrives-on

Good Reads. (n.d.-c). Organizing solutions for people with attention deficit disorder quotes by Susan C. Pinsky. Www.goodreads.com. https://www.goodreads.com/work/quotes/270582-organizing-solutions-for-people-with-attention-deficit-disorder-tips-an

Gowmon, V. (2019, May 29). Inspiring quotes on child learning and development. Vince Gowmon. https://www.vincegowmon.com/inspiring-quotes-on-child-learning-and-development/

Gwen. (2019, October 21). Calm and collected: 13 Stress relief activities for kids. Meraki Lane. https://www.merakilane.com/calm-and-collected-13-stress-relief-activities-for-kids/

Hart, A. (2022). 10 Lovely children's mental health quotes to inspire your kids. Twinkl https://www.twinkl.co.za/blog/10-lovely-childrens-mental-health-quotes-to-inspire-your-kids

Jen. (2020, March 21). 30 Fun ways to teach kids to be organized around the house. Organizenvy. https://organizenvy.com/kids-at-home/

Kingston, T. (2019, June 5). 45+ Fun physical activities for kids of all ages, categorized. Family Fun Twin Cities. https://www.familyfuntwincities.com/physical-activities-for-kids/

Kristenson, S. (2022, May 13). 11 Fun problem solving activities for kids. Develop Good Habits. https://www.developgoodhabits.com/problem-solving-kids/

MacDonald, F. (2015, April 20). Kids with ADHD need to move in order to learn, research reveals. ScienceAlert. https://www.sciencealert.com/kids-with-adhd-need-to-move-in-order-to-learn-research-reveals

Makvana, H. (2021, November 26). 20 Fun-filled indoor and outdoor activities for children with ADHD. MomJunction. https://www.momjunction.com/articles/good-activities-for-kids-with-adhd_00788965/

Marshall-Seslar, A. (2022, April 30). 60 Inspiring outdoor play quotes to get us all outside. Wellbeing with Alysia. https://wellbeingswithalysia.com/outdoor-play-quotes/

Miller, K. (2019, May 21). 39 Communication games and activities for kids, teens, and students. Positive Psychology. https://positivepsychology.com/communication-activities-adults-students/

Miracle Recreation. (2019, September 30). Why should my child play outside? Benefits of outdoor play for kids. Miracle Recreation. https://www.miracle-recreation.com/blog/why-should-my-child-play-outside-benefits-of-outdoor-play-for-kids/?lang=can

Morin, A. (2020, August 31). 15 Coping strategies for kids: Simple skills can help kids embrace their emotions. Verywell Family. https://www.verywellfamily.com/coping-skills-for-kids-4586871

Mum's Little Explorers. (2018, May 16). Kids need to get out and explore, they won't remember their best day of TV. Mum's Little Explorers. https://mumslittleexplorers.com/why-kids-need-to-get-out-and-explore/

Pacheco, D. (2021, January 8). How to build a better bedtime routine for adults. Sleep Foundation. https://www.sleepfoundation.org/sleep-hygiene/bedtime-routine-for-adults

Ratey, N. (2022, August 25). Keep calm and breathe om: 7 ADHD relaxation techniques. ADDitude. https://www.additudemag.com/adhd-relaxation-techniques-to-reduce-stress/

Ravi, A. (2022, September 22). 15 Fun activities to teach problem solving to kids. MomJunction. https://www.momjunction.com/articles/how-to-teach-problem-solving-for-kids-activities_00733680/

Reiff Ellis, R. (2020, September 12). What's the best exercise to manage ADHD symptoms? WebMD; WebMD. https://www.webmd.com/add-adhd/exercise-manage-adhd-symptoms

Rowley, B. (n.d.). 8 Fun games to end bedtime struggles. Parenting. https://www.parenting.com/toddler/8-fun-games-to-end-bedtime-struggles/

Sciberras, E. (2020, June). How can we help children with ADHD get a better night's sleep? CHADD. https://chadd.org/attention-article/how-can-we-help-children-with-adhd-get-a-better-nights-sleep/

Smith, J. (2021, June 29). Teaching your ADHD child home organization strategies. FastBraiin. https://www.fastbraiin.com/blogs/blog/adhd-teaching-your-child-home-organization-strategies

Sutcliffe, A. (2017, October 3). 14 Games to play before bed that guarantee a trip to dreamland. Tinybeans. https://tinybeans.com/bedtime-games-to-play-with-kids/

The Understood Team. (n.d.). Vacation ideas for very active kids. Www.understood.org. https://www.understood.org/en/articles/8-vacation-ideas-for-kids-with-adhd

Weelicious. (2021, October 16). 20 Easy recipes to make with your kids. Weelicious.com. https://weelicious.com/20-easy-recipes-to-make-with-your-kids/

Zhang, J. (2020, December 28). 65 ADHD quotes to help you understand it better. Emoovio. https://emoovio.com/adhd-quotes/

Image References

13Smok. (n.d.). Cat animal kitten tomcat pet [Online Image]. In Pixabay. https://pixabay.com/vectors/cat-animal-kitten-tomcat-pet-2722309/

Absteress. (n.d.). Hopscotch steps numbers two three [Online Image]. In Pixabay. https://pixabay.com/photos/hopscotch-steps-numbers-two-three-3878608/

Anderson, D. (2020). A family wearing a diy cardboard box mask [Online Image]. In Pexels. https://www.pexels.com/photo/a-family-wearing-a-diy-cardboard-box-mask-5589908/

ArtRose. (n.d.-a). Duckling hat easter house duck [Online Image]. In Pixabay. https://pixabay.com/vectors/duckling-hat-easter-house-duck-6122936/

ArtRose. (n.d.-b). Flowers daffodils bouquet spring [Online Image]. In Pixabay. https://pixabay.com/vectors/flowers-daffodils-bouquet-spring-6137354/

ArtsyBeeKids. (n.d.). Roller skates coloring book outline [Online Image]. In Pexels. https://pixabay.com/illustrations/roller-skates-coloring-book-outline-5639232/

Cameron, J. M. (2020). Woman in pink and yellow crew neck t-shirt holding brown notebook [Online Image]. In Pexels. https://www.pexels.com/photo/woman-in-pink-and-yellow-crew-neck-t-shirt-holding-brown-notebook-4143801/

Clker Free Vector Images. (n.d.). Raindrops funny characters cartoon [Online Image]. In Pixabay. https://pixabay.com/vectors/raindrops-funny-characters-cartoon-40997/

Cottonbro. (2020). Kids being goofy while making easter egg [Online Image]. In Pexels. https://www.pexels.com/photo/kids-being-goofy-while-making-easter-egg-3971485/

Danilyuk, P. (2021). Boy in red and gray long sleeves shirt sitting on floor while reaching for his toes [Online Image]. In Pexels. https://www.pexels.com/photo/boy-in-red-and-gray-long-sleeves-shirt-sitting-on-floor-while-reaching-for-his-toes-8422128/

de Richelieu, A. (2022). Mother and daughter preparing avocado toast [Online Image]. In Pexels. https://www.pexels.com/photo/mother-and-daughter-preparing-avocado-toast-4259707/

DreamDigitalArtist. (n.d.). Aircraft airplane drawing [Online Image]. In Pixabay. https://pixabay.com/vectors/aircraft-airplane-drawing-6769425/

Fairytale, E. (2020). Girl sleeping in bed [Online Image]. In Pexels. https://www.pexels.com/photo/girl-sleeping-in-bed-6202184/

Fring, G. (2020). Man in gray crew neck t-shirt and denim jeans wiping wooden floor [Online Image]. In Pexels. https://www.pexels.com/photo/man-in-gray-crew-neck-t-shirt-and-denim-jeans-wiping-wooden-floor-3890163/

Gambardella, J. (2020). Woman playing with two children [Online Image]. In Pexels. https://www.pexels.com/photo/woman-playing-with-two-children-6222766/

GDJ. (n.d.). Dog animal puppy baby canine [Online Image]. In Pixabay. https://pixabay.com/vectors/dog-animal-puppy-baby-canine-6387529/

Gorelova, T. (2020). A boy looking at the lighthouse [Online Image]. In Pexels. https://www.pexels.com/photo/a-boy-looking-at-the-lighthouse-3934194/

Kampus Production. (2021a). Children cooking food [Online Image]. In Pexels. https://www.pexels.com/photo/children-cooking-food-6481574/

Kampus Production. (2021b). A family having picnic [Online Image]. In Pexels. https://www.pexels.com/photo/a-family-having-a-picnic-7669130/

Kampus Production. (2022). Young girl putting sunscreen on a boy [Online Image]. In Pexels. https://www.pexels.com/photo/young-girl-putting-sunscreen-on-a-boy-8925992/

Kindel Media. (2021). Children playing in a room [Online Image]. In Pexels. https://www.pexels.com/photo/children-playing-in-a-room-7979779/

Krukov, Y. (2020). Child playing puzzle with mother at home [Online Image]. In Pexels. https://www.pexels.com/photo/child-playing-puzzle-with-mother-at-home-6210328/

Lach, R. (2021). Girl folding socks with her mother while sitting on floor [Online Image]. In Pexels. https://www.pexels.com/photo/girl-folding-socks-with-her-mother-while-sitting-on-floor-10557476/

Lenka, B. (n.d.). Clown circus fun coloring book [Online Image]. In Pixabay. https://pixabay.com/illustrations/clown-circus-fun-coloring-book-736058/

Mas, A. (2020). Interested little boy exploring stone [Online Image]. In Pexels. https://www.pexels.com/photo/interested-little-boy-exploring-stone-5623729/

Miroshnichenko, T. (2020). Mother and kids reading a book [Online Image]. In Pexels. https://www.pexels.com/photo/mother-and-kids-reading-a-book-5951842/

Monstera. (2021). Calm black kid meditating with closed eyes and mudra hands on bed [Online Image]. In Pexels. https://www.pexels.com/photo/calm-black-kid-meditating-with-closed-eyes-and-mudra-hands-on-bed-7353044/

Mortenson, N. (2021). Boy in blue and white striped polo shirt standing beside boy in pink polo shirt [Online Image]. In Pexels. https://www.pexels.com/photo/boy-in-blue-and-white-striped-polo-shirt-standing-beside-boy-in-pink-polo-shirt-8456153/

Open ClipArt Vectors. (n.d.). Horse horsemanship saddle animal [Online Image]. In Pixabay. https://pixabay.com/vectors/horse-horsemanship-saddle-animal-145443/

Open Clipart Vectors. (n.d.). Animal bunny ccc animals [Online Image]. In Pixabay. https://pixabay.com/vectors/animal-bunny-ccc-animals-1294930/

Piacquadio, A. (2020). Photo of girl holding ceramic cup [Online Image]. In Pexels. https://www.pexels.com/photo/photo-of-girl-holding-ceramic-cup-3890629/

Podrez, A. (2021). Woman in white shirt and blue denim shorts lying on bed [Online Image]. In Pexels. https://www.pexels.com/photo/woman-in-white-shirt-and-blue-denim-shorts-lying-on-bed-6941450/

Made in the USA
Monee, IL
15 September 2023

42798075R00050